Peekaboo! GOD Sees You!
Based on Psalm 139

By Theresa Perera

Every page has a little Special Star, can you find them all?

Peekaboo! GOD Sees You! - Based on Psalm 139

Written and designed by Theresa Perera
Editor: Jackie Pau
Contributor: Immanuel Perera

ISBN 978-1-7638095-1-2

Copyright 2024 by Theresa Perera
All rights reserved.
Thank you for purchasing an authorized edition of this book and for complying with copyright laws by not reproducing, scanning, storing in a retrieval system, or transmitting in any form, or by any means, electrical, mechanical, photocopying, recording or otherwise without the express written permission of the author and publisher except for the use of brief quotations in a book review.

www.TheresaPerera.com

*Deepest Gratitude to Almighty God
Who sees and knows us so deeply and
continues to love us so passionately.*

*To my Beloved Husband, my pillar of strength, my gift-from-God.
To our Precious son, our joy and blessing.*

Theresa Perera

Acknowledgement

I extend my deepest gratitude to my Editor, Jackie Pau, whose exceptional editorial skills and unwavering support have been instrumental in bringing this book to life. Your unique gift of finding meaning in few words has truly elevated this work.

I can see the Glory of God in you through your use of God-given talents. Your faithfulness as a Catholic has made a profound impact on this journey.

Thank you for believing in me and making this experience truly awesome.

Peekaboo! I See You!

I know you
through
and through.

I placed you inside your mummy

I saw you roll in her tummy

I love seeing you wake up and play

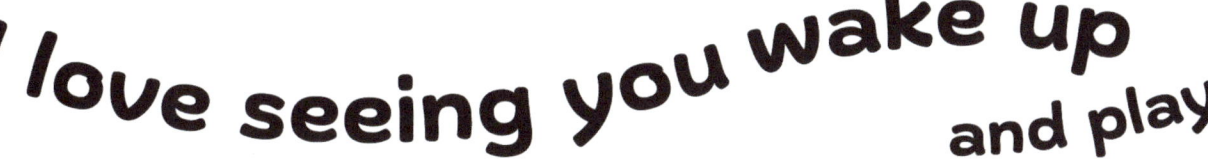

I even know
the dreams
you dream

I love you

even when you

scream !!

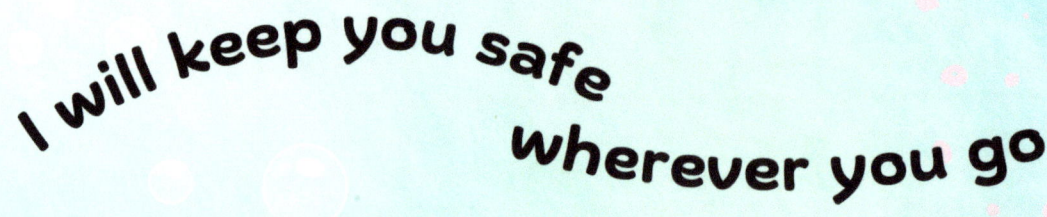

I will keep you safe wherever you go

I will watch over you give you space to grow

come wind, come snow.

I love you

more than
you ever will know.

Peekaboo! I See You!
and I LOVE you with all I've got.

Lots of Love,
from your Daddy

... And you are so precious to me.

Did you find all the Special Stars  in this book?

You are GOD's Special Star!
God made you Super Special! He blesses you in so many wonderful ways. Every day, when we look carefully at our lives, we can see these blessings, like finding stars in this book!

Prayer

Jesus, You are Loving and Good.
Teach me to love You as I should.

Jesus, you know when I sit and stand
Please hold me in Your Loving Hand

Jesus, You look after me day and night
You never leave me out of Your sight

Jesus, teach me to know You and to love You
For Your Ways are always Perfect and True

Jesus, help me follow in Your way
Guide me every day in what I do and say.

Amen.

About this story...

Psalm 139 proclaims God's immeasurable and intimate love. Despite turning away from God's love for 20 years, my life changed dramatically in 2000, when God's grace found me on my death bed and drew me back with His unfailing love. There's no looking back.

For the past nearly 25 years, I served in various ministries, sharing God's love and witnessing countless lives transformed. As a full time volunteer Missionary, I lived and worked in 5 countries. Together with my family, I have been running a YouTube channel for the past 4 years, hosting two live prayer meetings daily, praying with people around the world. Psalm 139 remains my guiding Scripture, a reminder of God's relentless pursuit after me. This story "Peekaboo, GOD sees you" has been my passion project. I hope it will help your child and many others come to know GOD's amazing love and mercy.

Your Review Helps Others

Write a Review on GoodReads

www.goodreads.com/book/show/221976064-peekaboo-god-sees-you

Enjoyed this book?
Please leave a **review on GoodReads or Amazon** or by scanning the QR Codes here —
your feedback is invaluable to me!

Your review encourages me to keep sharing my stories and helps others discover these books!
I sincerely appreciate your support.

Write a Review on Amazon

https://mybook.to/PeekabooBook

Free Activity Booklet
Instant Download on Website

www.TheresaPerera.com

www.ingramcontent.com/pod-product-compliance
Lightning Source LLC
Chambersburg PA
CBHW041704160426
43209CB00017B/1743